Guest Book To Celebrate

Thoughts / Messages

NAME:_____

NAME:_____

NAME:_____

NAME:_____

Thoughts / Messages

NAME:_____

NAME:_____

NAME:_____

NAME:_____

Thoughts / Messages

NAME:_____

NAME:_____

NAME:_____

NAME:_____

Thoughts / Messages

NAME:_____

NAME:_____

NAME:_____

NAME:_____

Thoughts / Messages

NAME:_____

NAME:_____

NAME:_____

NAME:_____

Thoughts / Messages

NAME:_____

NAME:_____

NAME:_____

NAME:_____

Thoughts / Messages

NAME:_____

NAME:_____

NAME:_____

NAME:_____

Thoughts / Messages

NAME:_____

NAME:_____

NAME:_____

NAME:_____

Thoughts / Messages

NAME:_____

NAME:_____

NAME:_____

NAME:_____

Thoughts / Messages

NAME:_____

NAME:_____

NAME:_____

NAME:_____

Thoughts / Messages

NAME:_____

NAME:_____

NAME:_____

NAME:_____

Thoughts / Messages

NAME:_____

NAME:_____

NAME:_____

NAME:_____

Thoughts / Messages

NAME:_____

NAME:_____

NAME:_____

NAME:_____

Thoughts / Messages

NAME:_____

NAME:_____

NAME:_____

NAME:_____

Thoughts / Messages

NAME:_____

NAME:_____

NAME:_____

NAME:_____

Thoughts / Messages

NAME:_____

NAME:_____

NAME:_____

NAME:_____

Thoughts / Messages

NAME:_____

NAME:_____

NAME:_____

NAME:_____

Thoughts / Messages

NAME:_____

NAME:_____

NAME:_____

NAME:_____

Thoughts / Messages

NAME:_____

NAME:_____

NAME:_____

NAME:_____

Thoughts / Messages

NAME:_____

NAME:_____

NAME:_____

NAME:_____

Thoughts / Messages

NAME:_____

NAME:_____

NAME:_____

NAME:_____

Thoughts / Messages

NAME:_____

NAME:_____

NAME:_____

NAME:_____

Thoughts / Messages

NAME:_____

NAME:_____

NAME:_____

NAME:_____

Thoughts / Messages

NAME:_____

NAME:_____

NAME:_____

NAME:_____

Thoughts / Messages

NAME:_____

NAME:_____

NAME:_____

NAME:_____

Thoughts / Messages

NAME:_____

NAME:_____

NAME:_____

NAME:_____

Thoughts / Messages

NAME:_____

NAME:_____

NAME:_____

NAME:_____

Thoughts / Messages

NAME:_____

NAME:_____

NAME:_____

NAME:_____

Thoughts / Messages

NAME:_____

NAME:_____

NAME:_____

NAME:_____

Thoughts / Messages

NAME:_____

NAME:_____

NAME:_____

NAME:_____

Thoughts / Messages

NAME:_____

NAME:_____

NAME:_____

NAME:_____

Thoughts / Messages

NAME:_____

NAME:_____

NAME:_____

NAME:_____

Thoughts / Messages

NAME:_____

NAME:_____

NAME:_____

NAME:_____

Thoughts / Messages

NAME:_____

NAME:_____

NAME:_____

NAME:_____

Thoughts / Messages

NAME:_____

NAME:_____

NAME:_____

NAME:_____

Thoughts / Messages

NAME:_____

NAME:_____

NAME:_____

NAME:_____

Thoughts / Messages

NAME:_____

NAME:_____

NAME:_____

NAME:_____

Thoughts / Messages

NAME:_____

NAME:_____

NAME:_____

NAME:_____

Thoughts / Messages

NAME:_____

NAME:_____

NAME:_____

NAME:_____

Thoughts / Messages

NAME:_____

NAME:_____

NAME:_____

NAME:_____

Thoughts / Messages

NAME:_____

NAME:_____

NAME:_____

NAME:_____

Thoughts / Messages

NAME:_____

NAME:_____

NAME:_____

NAME:_____

Thoughts / Messages

NAME:_____

NAME:_____

NAME:_____

NAME:_____

Thoughts / Messages

NAME:_____

NAME:_____

NAME:_____

NAME:_____

Thoughts / Messages

NAME:_____

NAME:_____

NAME:_____

NAME:_____

Thoughts / Messages

NAME:_____

NAME:_____

NAME:_____

NAME:_____

Thoughts / Messages

NAME:_____

NAME:_____

NAME:_____

NAME:_____

Thoughts / Messages

NAME:_____

NAME:_____

NAME:_____

NAME:_____

Thoughts / Messages

NAME:_____

NAME:_____

NAME:_____

NAME:_____

Thoughts / Messages

NAME:_____

NAME:_____

NAME:_____

NAME:_____

Thoughts / Messages

NAME:_____

NAME:_____

NAME:_____

NAME:_____

Thoughts / Messages

NAME:_____

NAME:_____

NAME:_____

NAME:_____

Thoughts / Messages

NAME:_____

NAME:_____

NAME:_____

NAME:_____

Thoughts / Messages

NAME:_____

NAME:_____

NAME:_____

NAME:_____

Thoughts / Messages

NAME:_____

NAME:_____

NAME:_____

NAME:_____

Thoughts / Messages

NAME:_____

NAME:_____

NAME:_____

NAME:_____

Thoughts / Messages

NAME:_____

NAME:_____

NAME:_____

NAME:_____

Thoughts / Messages

NAME:_____

NAME:_____

NAME:_____

NAME:_____

Thoughts / Messages

NAME:_____

NAME:_____

NAME:_____

NAME:_____

Thoughts / Messages

NAME:_____

NAME:_____

NAME:_____

NAME:_____

Thoughts / Messages

NAME:_____

NAME:_____

NAME:_____

NAME:_____

Thoughts / Messages

NAME:_____

NAME:_____

NAME:_____

NAME:_____

Thoughts / Messages

NAME:_____

NAME:_____

NAME:_____

NAME:_____

Thoughts / Messages

NAME:_____

NAME:_____

NAME:_____

NAME:_____

Thoughts / Messages

NAME:_____

NAME:_____

NAME:_____

NAME:_____

Thoughts / Messages

NAME:_____

NAME:_____

NAME:_____

NAME:_____

Thoughts / Messages

NAME:_____

NAME:_____

NAME:_____

NAME:_____

Thoughts / Messages

NAME:_____

NAME:_____

NAME:_____

NAME:_____

Thoughts / Messages

NAME:_____

NAME:_____

NAME:_____

NAME:_____

Thoughts / Messages

NAME:_____

NAME:_____

NAME:_____

NAME:_____

Thoughts / Messages

NAME:_____

NAME:_____

NAME:_____

NAME:_____

Thoughts / Messages

NAME:_____

NAME:_____

NAME:_____

NAME:_____

Thoughts / Messages

NAME:_____

NAME:_____

NAME:_____

NAME:_____

Thoughts / Messages

NAME:_____

NAME:_____

NAME:_____

NAME:_____

Thoughts / Messages

NAME:_____

NAME:_____

NAME:_____

NAME:_____

Thoughts / Messages

NAME:_____

NAME:_____

NAME:_____

NAME:_____

Thoughts / Messages

NAME:_____

NAME:_____

NAME:_____

NAME:_____

Thoughts / Messages

NAME:_____

NAME:_____

NAME:_____

NAME:_____

Thoughts / Messages

NAME:_____

NAME:_____

NAME:_____

NAME:_____

Thoughts / Messages

NAME:_____

NAME:_____

NAME:_____

NAME:_____

Thoughts / Messages

NAME:_____

NAME:_____

NAME:_____

NAME:_____

Thoughts / Messages

NAME:_____

NAME:_____

NAME:_____

NAME:_____

Thoughts / Messages

NAME:_____

NAME:_____

NAME:_____

NAME:_____

Thoughts / Messages

NAME:_____

NAME:_____

NAME:_____

NAME:_____

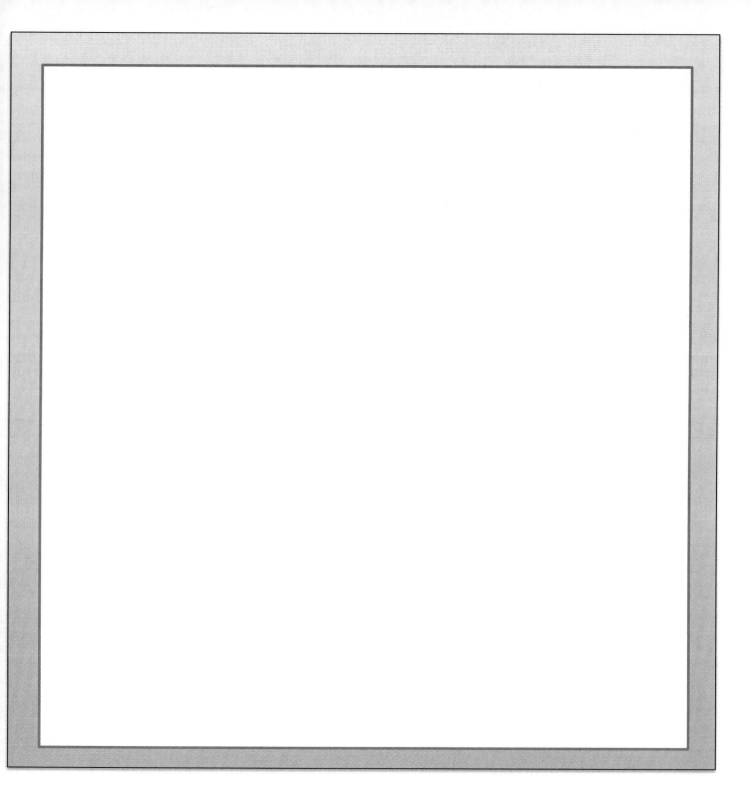

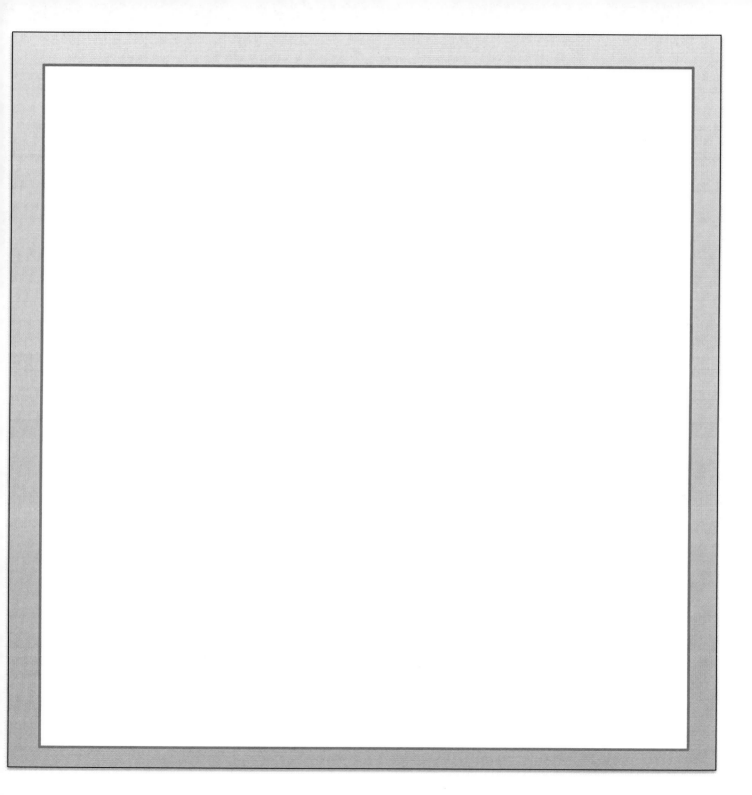

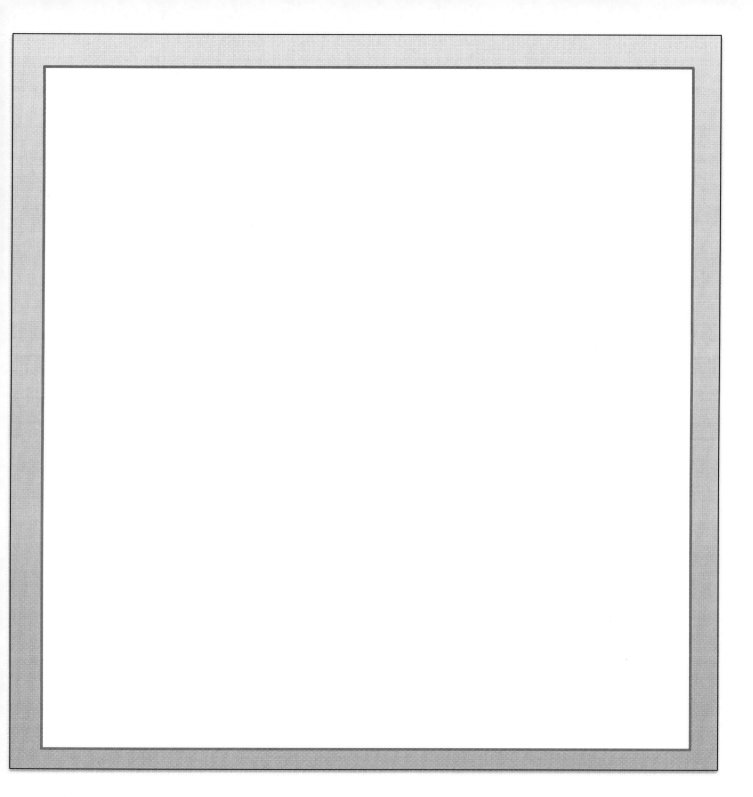

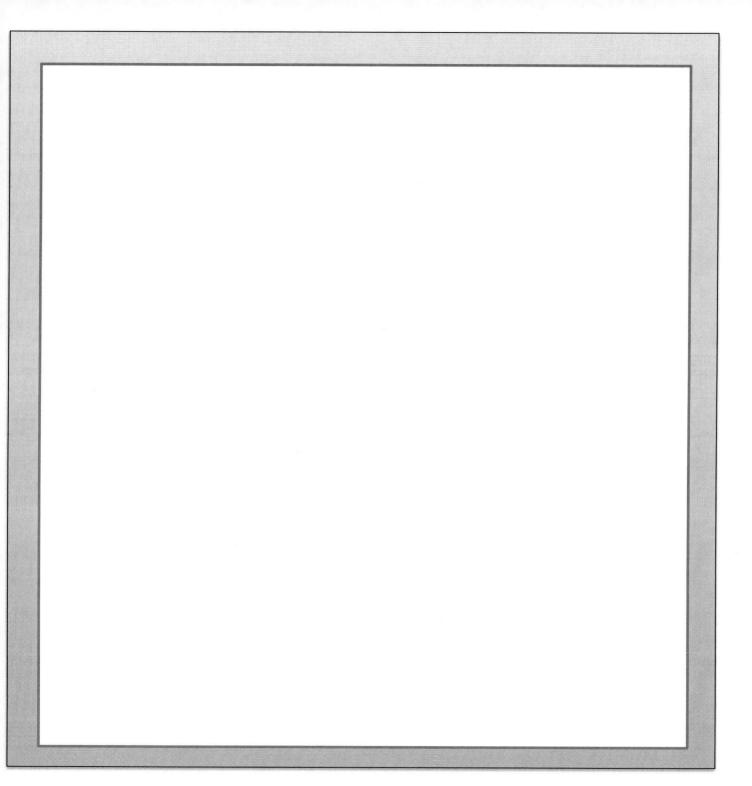

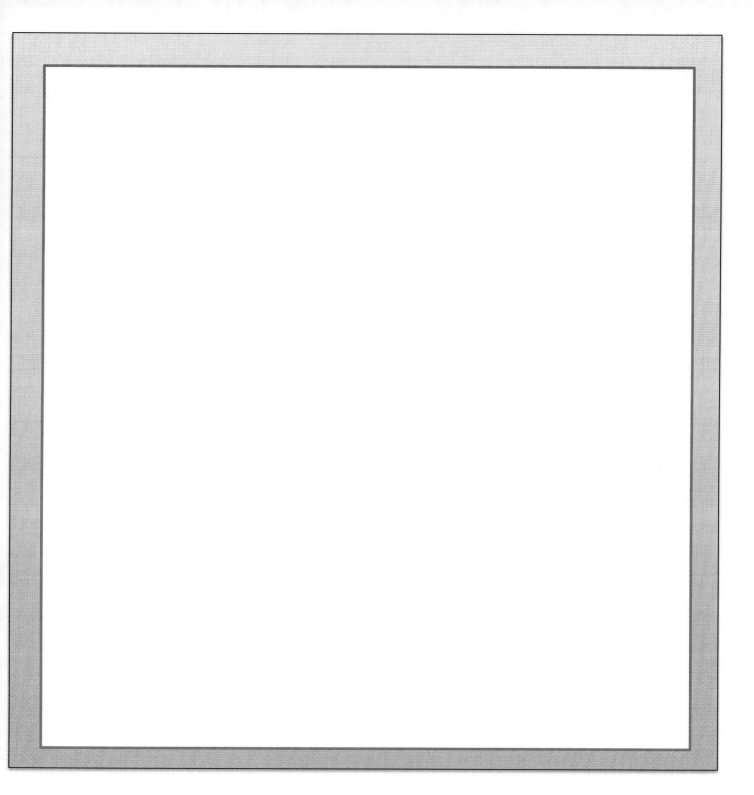

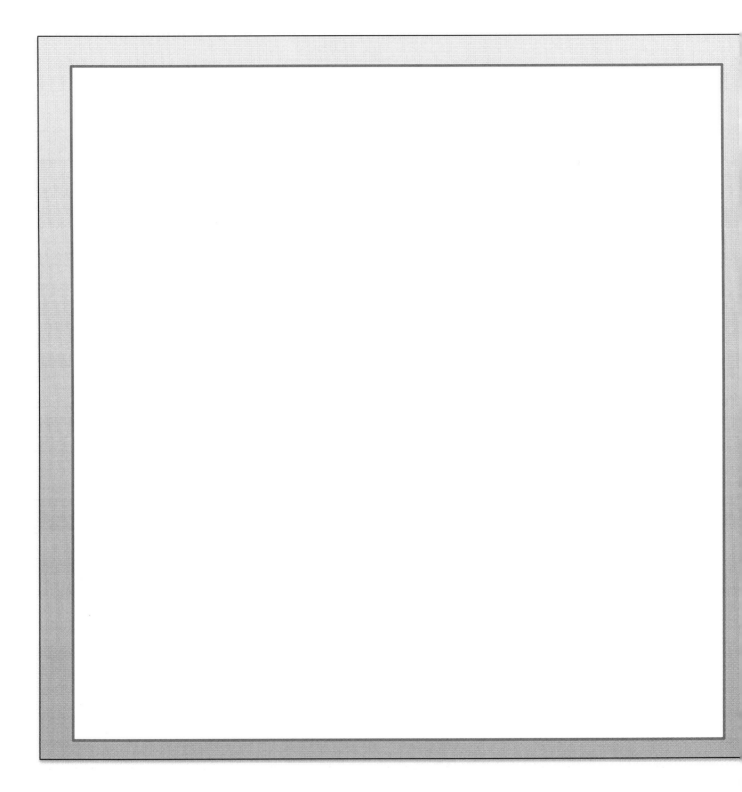

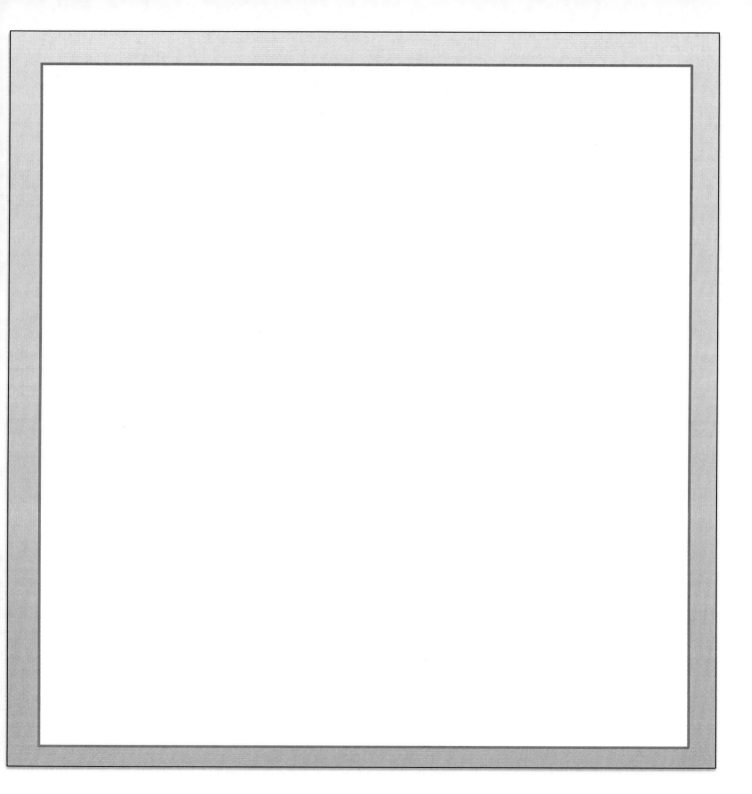

GIFT LOG

DATE	GIFT DESCRIPTION	GIVEN BY	THANK YOU NOTICE SENT

GIFT LOG

DATE	GIFT DESCRIPTION	GIVEN BY	THANK YOU NOTICE SENT

GIFT LOG

DATE	GIFT DESCRIPTION	GIVEN BY	THANK YOU NOTICE SENT

GIFT LOG

DATE	GIFT DESCRIPTION	GIVEN BY	THANK YOU NOTICE SENT

GIFT LOG

DATE	GIFT DESCRIPTION	GIVEN BY	THANK YOU NOTICE SENT

GIFT LOG

DATE	GIFT DESCRIPTION	GIVEN BY	THANK YOU NOTICE SENT

GIFT LOG

DATE	GIFT DESCRIPTION	GIVEN BY	THANK YOU NOTICE SENT

GIFT LOG

DATE	GIFT DESCRIPTION	GIVEN BY	THANK YOU NOTICE SENT

GIFT LOG

DATE	GIFT DESCRIPTION	GIVEN BY	THANK YOU NOTICE SENT

GIFT LOG

DATE	GIFT DESCRIPTION	GIVEN BY	THANK YOU NOTICE SENT

GIFT LOG

DATE	GIFT DESCRIPTION	GIVEN BY	THANK YOU NOTICE SENT

GIFT LOG

DATE	GIFT DESCRIPTION	GIVEN BY	THANK YOU NOTICE SENT

GIFT LOG

DATE	GIFT DESCRIPTION	GIVEN BY	THANK YOU NOTICE SENT

GIFT LOG

DATE	GIFT DESCRIPTION	GIVEN BY	THANK YOU NOTICE SENT

GIFT LOG

DATE	GIFT DESCRIPTION	GIVEN BY	THANK YOU NOTICE SENT

GIFT LOG

DATE	GIFT DESCRIPTION	GIVEN BY	THANK YOU NOTICE SENT

94620092R00064

Made in the USA
Middletown, DE
20 October 2018